The Ultimate Wilderness Survival Guide for Kids

Learning how to proficiently build fires, administer first aid, craft shelters, forage for resources, procure water, and other essential skills crucial for thriving in outdoor survival situations.

Ben Jason

TABLE OF CONTENT

Introduction

Welcome to The Ultimate Wilderness Survival Guide for Kids! Embracing the wild and thriving amidst nature's challenges can offer children an exhilarating, empowering, and educational experience. This guide is your gateway to essential knowledge and skills necessary to confront wilderness obstacles head-on.

Surviving in the wilderness encompasses more than mere survival – it fosters self-reliance, a deeper connection with nature, and lifesaving abilities applicable beyond survival scenarios. With the right mindset and proper training, any child can become adept at wilderness survival.

Within these pages, you'll delve into an array of techniques used by wilderness experts. Crucial topics like fire making, shelter construction, food foraging, water sourcing and purification, navigation, first aid, tools, hazard avoidance, and the essential survival mindset will be explored.

Equipped with this knowledge, you'll be ready to plan wilderness trips, handle emergencies, and develop long-term survival skills. The guide also outlines safe methods to bolster your training through supervised practical exercises.

Wilderness survival cultivates confidence, resilience, problem-solving, and invaluable life skills, reconnecting us with our primal origins and fostering a deep bond with nature. This handbook aims to make wilderness survival accessible to kids from diverse backgrounds and varying experience levels.

Get prepared for an adventurous journey into the wild! Through the training provided in this handbook, you'll not just survive but thrive in the wilderness. Let's embark on this exciting expedition!

An Extensive Overview of Wilderness Survival Basics

ATTIRE AND EQUIPMENT

The right attire and gear significantly impact your wilderness experience. Essential clothing comprises moisture-wicking fabrics, insulating layers, waterproof outerwear, and suitable footwear for the terrain. Vital gear includes a knife, fire starters, first aid kit, map, compass, cordage, shelter material, water container, and purification supplies. Opt for versatile, sturdy items adaptable to the climate, terrain, and duration of your adventure.

ENVIRONMENTAL AWARENESS

Familiarize yourself with the local flora, fauna, terrain, and climate. This understanding helps identify hazards, food sources, and ideal camping spots. Utilize field guides, maps, wildlife resources, and learn to predict weather through natural indicators like cloud patterns.

SKILL DEVELOPMENT

Real wilderness proficiency stems from practical experience. Practice fire building, shelter crafting, foraging, navigation, and other hands-on skills. Initiate in controlled environments, such as backyard camping, before progressing to more immersive settings. Mastery takes time but builds the instinctual muscle memory crucial for skill application.

SURVIVAL MINDSET

Confront any survival challenge with the right mindset. Remain observant, alert, and focused. Combat panic by logical thinking before action. Exercise patience, determination, and creativity in problem-solving. Search for opportunities and available resources. Trust in your capability to endure any hardship.

Establishing a robust foundation with these fundamentals sets the stage for expanding your wilderness capabilities. Absorb these core competencies, and you'll possess the confidence to explore the wild expanses.

Creating a Survival Kit with Essential Items

Crafting a survival kit with necessary items is a crucial skill for children preparing for wilderness adventures. Providing them with the knowledge to assemble a comprehensive survival kit ensures readiness for unexpected situations. Here's a detailed breakdown:

UNDERSTANDING ESSENTIAL COMPONENTS

Key items to include in the survival kit:

- **First Aid Supplies:** Bandages, antiseptic wipes, tweezers, and any essential medications for allergies or existing conditions.

- **Water Purification Tools:** Water purification tablets, a portable filter, or a small bottle of chlorine bleach for emergency water treatment.

- **Fire-Starting Materials**: Waterproof matches, a fire starter, or a lighter in a waterproof container.

- **Shelter and Protection**: A lightweight emergency blanket, a sturdy poncho, or a compact tarp for shelter.

- **Signaling Devices**: A whistle, a signal mirror, or a flashlight for attracting attention.

- **Multi-tool or Knife**: A child-friendly, small-sized multi-tool or knife for various tasks.

CUSTOMIZATION AND PERSONALIZATION

Steps to tailor the kit:

- **Discussing Needs**: Engage children in discussions about specific needs or situations they might encounter to customize the kit accordingly. For instance, including medications for allergies or insect bites.

- **Personal Touch:** Encourage personalization by allowing them to add a small note or comforting item to the kit.

Assembling the Kit

Guidelines for assembling the survival kit:

- **Demonstration and Guidance:** Step-by-step instructions on assembling the kit, explaining the purpose of each item. Emphasize proper storage and organization within a compact, waterproof container or pouch.

- **Practice Makes Perfect:** Allow children to practice packing and unpacking the kit, ensuring they grasp the placement and significance of each item.

MAINTENANCE AND REVIEW

Ensuring the kit stays functional and updated:

- **Regular Checks:** Stress the importance of periodic checks to ensure all items are in good condition and not expired.

- **Relevant Updates:** Update the kit as needed based on changing needs or seasonal considerations.

SAFETY GUIDELINES

Crucial safety measures and protocols:

- **Safety Rules:** Emphasize responsible handling of tools and seeking adult assistance when necessary.

- **Emergency Protocol:** Instruct children on when and how to use items in the kit, emphasizing that it's strictly for emergency situations.

Empowering children to create their survival kits not only equips them with practical skills but also enhances their confidence and readiness for outdoor adventures.

Navigating with a Compass and Reading Maps

Acquiring proficiency in using a compass and reading maps is a valuable skill for navigating the wilderness. Here's a comprehensive guide to assist in understanding, practicing, and enhancing these essential navigation tools:

UNDERSTANDING THE COMPASS

Compass Basics:

- A compass is a navigation tool with a needle that consistently points north when held flat and steady.

Cardinal Directions:

- Remember the main directions: North, South, East, and West, with the mnemonic "Never Eat Soggy Waffles."

READING MAPS

Map Overview:

- A map serves as a visual representation of the area, depicting features such as mountains, roads, and landmarks.

SYMBOLS AND LEGENDS:

- Maps utilize symbols to represent elements like roads, rivers, or mountains, explained in the map legend.

BASIC NAVIGATION SKILLS

Compass Direction:

- Align the compass needle with the north arrow to match the map with your surroundings.

Follow a Bearing:

- Choose a compass direction and walk while keeping the needle aligned with the north arrow.

PRACTICAL APPLICATION

Practice Outside:

- Utilize the compass and map in a park or open area to find landmarks or follow a planned trail.

Fun Games:

- Create engaging games using the map and compass, such as hiding an item marked on the map and using compass directions to find it.

SAFETY AND PRECAUTIONS

Stay Aware:

- Regularly check the compass while exploring to maintain awareness of your location and direction.

Safety Rules:

- Always carry a map and inform someone of your whereabouts. Stay composed if uncertain about your location and avoid wandering off.

ADVANCED TECHNIQUES

Learning More:

- As confidence grows, explore advanced techniques like adjusting for declination or understanding various map types.

SIMPLE MAP ACTIVITY FOR PRACTICE

Materials Needed:

- A straightforward map of a local park, hiking trail, or open area.

- A basic compass.

Steps:

1. **Study the Map:**

   - Familiarize yourself with map symbols and identify your location and landmarks.

2. **Map Orientation:**

   - Ensure the map aligns with the actual north direction around you.

3. **Compass Alignment:**

   - Hold the compass flat and align the needle with the north arrow on the map.

4. **Pick a Destination:**

   - Select a point on the map and determine its direction using the compass.

5. **Navigate:**

   - Walk toward the chosen point while keeping the compass needle aligned with the north arrow. Periodically check the map to ensure the correct direction.

6. **Reach Your Destination:**

   - Celebrate upon successfully reaching the designated point!

Remember to practice consistently to build confidence. As your skills progress, consider exploring diverse maps and attempting more challenging activities. Enjoy the thrill of discovering new places using your map and compass skills!

Identifying Safe and Unsafe Plants

When it comes to wilderness survival, understanding which plants are safe to consume and which are potentially harmful is a crucial skill for children. This knowledge lays the foundation for their safety and well-being in natural environments. Here's an in-depth exploration:

UNDERSTANDING SAFE PLANTS

Teaching children about safe, edible plants involves imparting knowledge about their visual characteristics, sensory cues, and positive identification methods:

- **Visual Characteristics:** Children should be familiarized with the appearance of common edible plants, emphasizing details such as leaf shapes, colors, and textures. It's essential to highlight easily recognizable edible plants like dandelions, various berries, or wild onions.

- **Sensory Cues:** Encourage children to use their senses when identifying safe plants. Some edible plants have distinct smells or identifiable features, such as recognizable fruits or nuts.

- **Positive Identification:** Guide children in cautiously identifying edible plants through multiple identifying features. Utilize resources like guidebooks or user-friendly plant identification apps to reinforce their learning.

RECOGNIZING UNSAFE PLANTS

Educating children about potentially harmful plants and emphasizing caution in plant consumption is vital:

- **Common Poisonous Plants:** Introduce children to common poisonous plants in the local area. Emphasize features that distinguish these plants from safe ones, such as unusual coloration, distinct markings, or strong odors.

- **Teaching Caution:** Stress the critical rule of never consuming any plant without proper identification or adult supervision. Teach them the adage "when in doubt, leave it out" as a safety measure.

Hands-on Learning

Engaging children in practical activities and interactive learning experiences can enhance their understanding of safe and unsafe plants:

- **Field Trips and Practical Activities:** Organize nature walks or field trips where children can observe and identify safe plants under guidance. Activities such as creating a plant identification booklet or scavenger hunts for edible plants can be both enjoyable and educational.

- **Interactive Learning Tools:** Utilize visual aids, flashcards, or engaging plant identification apps to immerse children in interactive learning experiences.

Safety Measures

Instilling safety measures and guidelines around plant identification and consumption is crucial for their well-being:

- **Establishing Rules:** Set clear rules regarding foraging or consuming plants in the wild, emphasizing caution and the importance of seeking adult guidance.

- **Encouraging Doubt and Caution:** Teach children to exercise caution and doubt their plant identification skills unless they are completely confident. Reinforce that it's perfectly fine not to consume something if they are uncertain about its safety.

By providing children with the knowledge and skills to differentiate between safe and unsafe plants, we equip them with an invaluable survival skill that fosters confidence, curiosity, and a profound respect for the natural world.

RECOGNIZING DANGEROUS WILDLIFE AND THEIR BEHAVIORS

Understanding potentially dangerous wildlife and learning how to interact with or avoid them is pivotal for ensuring wilderness safety. Educating children about potential threats and appropriate behavior around wildlife not only promotes safety but also nurtures a deeper appreciation for nature. Here's a more comprehensive look at this crucial aspect:

UNDERSTANDING ANIMAL BEHAVIOR

Equipping children with knowledge about local dangerous wildlife behaviors is essential:

- **Species Awareness:** Introduce children to dangerous local wildlife, focusing on animals like snakes, bears, cougars, or venomous insects. Highlight their habitats, behaviors, and warning signs.

- **Signs of Aggression:** Educate children on recognizing signs of aggression or distress in wildlife, emphasizing the importance of slowly backing away if they observe these behaviors.

SAFE INTERACTIONS AND DISTANCE

Teaching children about maintaining a safe distance and being cautious around wildlife is paramount:

- **Maintaining Distance:** Explain the concept of a "safe distance" when encountering wildlife. Encourage observing animals from a distance and avoiding direct approaches or attempts to touch or feed them.

- **Teaching Caution:** Instill caution in children when encountering wildlife, emphasizing that not all animals are approachable or friendly.

STRATEGIES FOR ENCOUNTERS

Preparing children with appropriate reactions and strategies for encounters with dangerous wildlife is crucial:

- **Reacting to Encounters:** Discuss appropriate reactions when encountering dangerous wildlife, such as staying calm, slowly backing away, and making themselves appear larger (in the case of bears or cougars).

- **Group Safety:** Emphasize the importance of sticking together in groups while exploring the wilderness, as animals might be less likely to approach larger groups.

RESPECT AND CONSERVATION

Nurturing respect and awareness for wildlife conservation is integral to fostering a sense of responsibility:

- **Respectful Observance:** Educate children about respecting wildlife by observing from a distance and avoiding interference in their natural behaviors.

- **Conservation Awareness:** Instill a sense of conservation and the significance of preserving wildlife habitats. Explain how

respecting animals' space contributes to
their conservation.

Interactive Learning

Utilizing engaging and interactive learning methods
can reinforce understanding and preparedness:

- **Visual Learning Tools**: Incorporate visuals,
  videos, or wildlife documentaries showcasing
  animal behaviors and interactions in their
  natural habitats.

- **Role-playing and Scenarios**: Engage
  children in role-playing scenarios simulating
  wildlife encounters, allowing them to
  practice appropriate reactions and
  responses.

Empowering children with knowledge about
potentially dangerous wildlife and their behaviors
not only ensures their safety but also instills
empathy and respect for the natural world's
delicate balance.

Reading Weather Signs for Wilderness Survival

Mastering the ability to read weather signs is a pivotal skill for children venturing into the wilderness. This knowledge empowers them to anticipate and prepare for changes in weather conditions, ensuring their safety. Here's an in-depth exploration:

CLOUD FORMATIONS

Understanding cloud types and their implications for weather changes:

- **Cloud Types:** Teach children about various cloud types like cumulus, cirrus, and stratus. For instance, cumulonimbus clouds often signal thunderstorms.

- **Observation Skills:** Encourage regular observation of cloud formations, noting changes in shape, color, or movement that might indicate impending weather changes.

Wind Patterns

Comprehending wind and its relationship with upcoming weather changes:

- **Understanding Wind**: Educate children on how wind direction indicates potential weather shifts. Explain how changes in wind patterns might suggest alterations in weather conditions.

- **Experiments**: Conduct simple experiments using wind socks or other tools to demonstrate wind direction and its influence on weather changes.

CHANGES IN AIR PRESSURE

Explaining the concept of barometric pressure and its link to weather changes:

- **Barometric Pressure**: Introduce the concept and its association with weather changes. Encourage observation of pressure changes using basic barometers or improvised methods.

- **Relating to Weather Changes**: Teach children that abrupt shifts in barometric pressure often precede weather events like storms or temperature shifts.

NATURAL INDICATORS

Utilizing natural indicators to predict weather events:

- **Animal Behavior:** Discuss how animals might behave differently before a weather event, such as birds seeking shelter before a storm. Observing these behaviors serves as indicators.

- **Natural Cues:** Educate children about natural cues like changes in sky color, humidity levels, or the behavior of insects that might precede weather changes.

PREDICTING WEATHER EVENTS

Enhancing observation skills for predicting weather changes:

- **Keeping Records:** Encourage children to maintain weather observation journals or logs. This habit helps them recognize patterns and improves their ability to predict weather changes.

- **Real-Life Examples:** Share anecdotes or real-life instances where weather signs accurately predicted changes, emphasizing the importance of paying attention to nature's signals.

INTERACTIVE LEARNING

Engaging in practical outdoor observations to reinforce learning:

- **Outdoor Observations:** Organize outdoor sessions where children actively observe and identify weather signs in real-time. Hands-on experiences in the natural environment reinforce learning and make it practical.

Empowering children with the ability to read weather signs not only enhances their self-reliance and preparedness in the wilderness but also deepens their connection with the natural world, promoting safety and environmental awareness.

Navigating by the Stars and Natural Signs

Navigating using the stars and natural signs is an ancient yet fascinating method for finding direction in the wilderness. Let's explore this topic in a beginner-friendly manner:

UNDERSTANDING THE STARS

Identify Major Constellations:

- Recognize easily visible constellations like the Big Dipper, Orion, or Cassiopeia, which act as celestial landmarks guiding your way.

Polaris - the North Star:

- Polaris, known as the North Star, serves as a steady reference point. Find it by drawing an imaginary line through the two outer stars of the Big Dipper's bowl, pointing nearly due north.

OBSERVING NATURAL SIGNS

Sun's Path:

- The sun rises in the east, sets in the west, and at noon, shadows are shortest and point toward the north in the northern hemisphere.

Moss and Trees:

- Moss tends to grow more on the north side of trees in the northern hemisphere due to reduced sunlight, offering a general indicator of direction.

BASIC CELESTIAL NAVIGATION

Using Constellations as Guides:

- Understanding the movement of constellations, like the Big Dipper rotating around Polaris, helps gauge direction throughout the night.

Southern Hemisphere Navigation:

- In the southern hemisphere, the Southern Cross constellation is crucial for finding south, with its longer axis pointing to the south celestial pole.

PRACTICAL APPLICATION

Starry Night Observations:

- Practice stargazing on clear nights. Identify learned constellations and observe their positions relative to each other.

Nighttime Strolls:

- During supervised nighttime walks, use stars as guides. Try finding the North Star or identifying prominent constellations for direction.

SAFETY AND LIMITATIONS

Safety Measures:

- Navigate in safe environments, especially during nighttime practices, ensuring adult supervision.

Understanding Limitations:

- Recognize that weather conditions or landscape may hinder visibility or accuracy of natural signs and stars. Consider them as supplementary navigation aids.

IDENTIFYING KEY CONSTELLATIONS FOR NAVIGATION

The Big Dipper (Ursa Major):

- Recognize the group of seven stars forming a "ladle" shape in the northern sky.

- Note that the two outer stars in the "bowl" point to the North Star, Polaris, acting as a reliable marker for north.

Orion:

- Identify Orion with three stars forming his belt.

- Follow an imaginary line through Orion's belt to find Sirius, the brightest star in the sky, generally seen in the south during winter evenings.

Cassiopeia:

Notice Cassiopeia's "W" or "M" shape in the northern sky.

Use Cassiopeia to locate the North Star by drawing an imaginary line from its top peak or bottom dip.

Southern Cross (Crux) for Southern Hemisphere:

Look for a cross-shaped constellation where the longer axis points toward the southern celestial pole, indicating the south direction.

Practice Activity:

Spot constellations on a clear night using a sky map or stargazing app. Observe their positions relative to each other, learning how they change throughout the night.

Using Natural Signs for Direction

Sun's Path:

Observe sunrise and sunset to determine east and west. At noon, the sun is south (northern hemisphere) or north (southern hemisphere).

Shadows:

In the morning, shadows extend westward, and in the afternoon, they shift toward the east.

Moss on Trees:

Moss growth on the north side of trees (in the northern hemisphere) is a general indicator of direction but may not always be accurate.

Wind and Weather Patterns:

Consistent prevailing winds or weather patterns can indicate direction, like storm clouds coming from a specific direction.

Landmarks and Natural Features:

Rivers and mountain ranges can guide direction, with rivers often flowing consistently and mountains serving as long-term reference points.

Practical Application

Hands-On Observations:

During hikes, note natural signs and their changes based on time or season.

Map Comparison:

Compare observed natural features with maps while hiking, correlating landscape features with map indications.

Safety Considerations

Environmental Awareness:

Natural signs may not always be visible or reliable due to weather changes or local variations.

Supplement with Other Tools:

Use natural signs alongside maps or compasses for more accurate navigation.

Using a GPS device or a smartphone app for navigation

Using a GPS device or a smartphone app for navigation presents a modern and accessible way to traverse the wilderness. This guide aims to introduce beginners to this method:

GPS BASICS EXPLAINED:

Understanding GPS:

GPS, or Global Positioning System, utilizes satellites to precisely pinpoint your location on Earth. These satellites transmit signals to your GPS device or smartphone app.

Using a Smartphone App:

SELECTING A NAVIGATION APP:

- Choose a reputable GPS navigation app compatible with your smartphone's operating system, such as Google Maps, Apple Maps, Gaia GPS, or ViewRanger.

DOWNLOAD AND INSTALL THE APP FROM YOUR DEVICE'S APP STORE.

Operating the GPS Device or App:

Activating the GPS Function:

- Enable the GPS function in your device's settings or permissions to allow the navigation app access to your location.

- Open the navigation app and grant access to location services if prompted.

Setting Destinations and Routes:

- Input your desired destination or set waypoints using the search or address function within the app.

- Follow the app's instructions to establish a route or select a destination.

UNDERSTANDING NAVIGATION FEATURES:

- **Turn-by-Turn Directions**: The app provides step-by-step guidance through spoken instructions and visual maps, leading you to your destination.

- **Additional Features:** Explore supplementary features like offline maps, satellite imagery, elevation profiles, or trail maps based on the app's capabilities. Customize settings such as map orientation or voice guidance.

Practical Application:

Practice in Familiar Areas:

- Initiate usage in familiar environments or short trips to acquaint yourself with the app's functions and interface.

Safety and Battery Considerations:

- Ensure your device is fully charged, especially in remote areas where recharging might be impossible.

- Carry backup batteries or a power bank as GPS usage can rapidly drain a smartphone's battery.

REVIEW AND EXPLORATION:

Review and Learn:

- Reflect on your experience using the app, noting its accuracy and identifying any overlooked features or settings.

Using a navigation app during outdoor expeditions can be advantageous. Here's an expanded guide for utilizing a navigation app during your wilderness adventure:

USING A NAVIGATION APP DURING YOUR OUTDOOR ADVENTURE:

1. Choose and Download the App:

Selection Process:

- Access the app store on your device (Google Play Store for Android or Apple App Store for iOS).

- Search for a reliable navigation app like Google Maps, Gaia GPS, or ViewRanger, then install it.

2. Familiarize Yourself with the App:

App Settings:

- Explore the app's features and locate options to customize settings like map view, route preferences, or voice guidance.

- Learn how to download maps for offline usage in areas with poor network coverage.

3. Planning Your Route:

Setting Destinations:

- Input your starting point and desired destination.

- Review and select the route that aligns with your preferences.

4. Using the App During Your Adventure:

Activation and Navigation:

- Enable GPS and launch the navigation app.

- Follow the app's instructions for navigation, paying attention to map displays and turn-by-turn directions or spoken guidance.

5. Exploration and Utilizing Features:

Exploring Map Views:

- Experiment with different map views (satellite, terrain, or standard) to comprehend the landscape.

- Utilize extra features like trail maps, waypoints, or specific outdoor functionalities offered by the app.

6. Safety and Battery Management:

Safety Awareness:

- Prioritize safety, remaining attentive to surroundings and any trail markers or natural signs.

- Always carry a backup map and compass in case of technical issues or battery depletion.

Battery Conservation:

- Optimize battery usage by adjusting screen brightness, closing unused apps, or activating battery-saving modes.

- Consider carrying a portable charger or power bank for recharging.

7. Post-Adventure Review:

Reflect and Learn:

- Evaluate the app's performance during your adventure. Note challenges faced or features that proved particularly beneficial.

- Use this experience to refine your navigation skills with the app for future adventures.

Utilizing a navigation app is both practical and enjoyable. Remember, while it serves as a valuable tool, combining it with traditional navigation skills enhances your wilderness experience.

Constructing Shelters in the Wilderness

Constructing shelters in the wilderness is a crucial skill for children exploring the outdoors. This guide aims to equip them with the knowledge to build secure shelters, covering aspects like material selection, optimal site identification, and the construction process.

THE IMPORTANCE OF SHELTER CONSTRUCTION

Understanding shelter construction's critical nature in the wild is fundamental. A lack of expertise or tools can expose children to elements, risks, or injury. Building a shelter provides refuge and safety in the wilderness.

SELECTING AN IDEAL SITE

Key Considerations:

- **Safety**: Protection from threats like predators or harsh weather is crucial.

- **Resources**: Proximity to water, food, and materials for sustainability.

- **Terrain**: Flat ground, sheltered from elements, devoid of obstacles is ideal.

Optimal Location:

- Seek areas shielded by trees, rocks, or hills for protection.

- Ensure access to water, food, and ample construction materials.

- Choose flat terrain with minimal obstacles for easy construction.

CONTEMPLATING SHELTER TYPE

Crafting the Shelter:

- Determine the type based on available resources and protection needs.

- Options range from lean-tos to more complex structures with walls and roofs.

VIGILANCE DURING SITE SELECTION

Safety Measures:

Survey the area for wildlife or hazardous plants.

Be vigilant about signs of human activity or potential dangers in the surroundings.

GATHERING ESSENTIAL MATERIALS FOR SHELTER CONSTRUCTION

Gathering essential materials is crucial for a successful shelter construction process. Here's a breakdown of the materials needed:

Frame Materials:

Sturdy Material: Robust wood, bamboo, or substantial branches for the frame's stability and weight-bearing capacity.

Smaller Wood Pieces and Twigs: Essential for constructing the walls.

Rocks: Required for stabilizing and supporting the structure.

Shelter Covering:

Waterproof Material: A tarp, blanket, or canvas to shield against the elements.

Rope or String: Necessary for securing the covering to the frame.

Tools:

Saw or Hammer: For shaping wood and pounding.

Knife: Useful for cutting rope, trimming covering, and various tasks.

Insulation and Wall Filling:

Leaves, Grass, Moss, Tree Bark: Insulation materials for filling gaps between walls, providing warmth and structural integrity.

CONSTRUCTION PROCESS:

BUILDING A SHELTER

1. Building the Frame

Gather Materials: Collect long, robust sticks, branches, and vines of similar lengths.

Assemble the Frame: Cut sticks to uniform lengths and securely tie them at corners to form a sturdy rectangular frame.

Secure the Frame: Use additional materials like vines to reinforce the corners and other areas for structural support.

Construct the Shelter: Fashion an A-frame roof using additional branches and cover it with leaves or natural materials for insulation and protection.

2. Adding Insulation for Comfort and Protection

Collect Insulation Materials: Utilize grasses, pine needles, leaves, moss, or dried reeds.

Line the Walls: Layer insulation materials along the shelter's inner walls, using a mix of grass, pine needles, and moss for effective insulation.

Create Warm Air Traps: Pile pine needles and leaves around the shelter walls to trap warm air inside.

Consider Supplementary Coverings: Add an extra blanket or sleeping bag for additional warmth and insulation.

COVERING AND COMFORT FOR THE SHELTER

Covering the Shelter

After constructing the shelter frame and insulating it, the next crucial step is covering it adequately for protection against wind and rain. Here's a detailed process:

1. **Material Collection:** Gather thin, flexible branches and leaves from nearby trees and bushes.

2. **Placement**: Begin from the shelter's base, layering branches and leaves around the frame in an overlapping pattern, creating a strong barrier against wind and rain.

3. **Securing the Cover**: Fasten branches tightly to the shelter's frame using string, twine, or nails for added security, ensuring a snug fit to prevent displacement.

4. **Closing Gaps**: Fill any gaps in the shelter frame with branches and leaves to further fortify it against wind and rain.

5. **Mulch Application**: Add a layer of mulch on top to enhance insulation and keep the shelter dry.

Making the Shelter Comfortable

For additional warmth and comfort:

1. **Insulation Materials**: Gather easily layered materials like leaves, grasses, and moss, known for heat retention and effective insulation.

2. **Creating a Mattress:** Layer leaves, grasses, and moss on the ground, followed by softer padding materials like pine needles or bark for a comfortable sleeping space.

3. **Sealing the Shelter:** Use small branches and twigs to cover shelter edges, preventing drafts and ensuring coziness throughout the night.

SAFETY CONSIDERATIONS FOR SHELTER CONSTRUCTION

Ensuring safety is paramount during shelter construction. Here are key safety considerations to remember:

1. **Inform Someone:** Share your location and activity details with someone trustworthy.

2. **Bring Necessary Supplies:** Carry the tools and materials required for shelter construction.

3. **Remain Vigilant:** Stay alert for potential dangers like wildlife or hazardous conditions.

4. **Weather Awareness**: Stay updated on the weather forecast and be prepared for sudden changes.

5. **Know Your Limits**: Work within your capabilities to avoid overexertion.

6. **Dress Appropriately**: Wear weather-appropriate clothing for protection.

7. **Take Breaks**: Rest when necessary to avoid exhaustion.

8. **Fire Safety**: If using a campfire, ensure it's safely managed and extinguished.

9. **Stay Hydrated**: Drink enough water to remain hydrated.

10. **Leave No Trace**: Respect the environment and leave the area clean.

Staying Warm and Dry in Different Weather Conditions

Proper Clothing for Weather Conditions:

- **Layering Technique:**

    - **Base Layer:** Wear moisture-wicking clothing (polyester, merino wool) to keep sweat away from the skin.

    - **Insulating Layer:** Use fleece or wool to trap body heat.

    - **Outer Layer:** Invest in a waterproof and windproof jacket or shell to protect against rain, snow, and wind.

Fire for Warmth:

- **Basic Fire-Starting Techniques:**

    - **Carry Fire-Starting Tools:** Keep matches, lighters, or fire starters in a waterproof container.

- **Firewood Preparation:** Collect dry wood, kindling, and tinder before starting a fire.

Shelter and Insulation:

- **Well-Built Shelter:**

  - Construct a shelter using natural materials to shield against wind and precipitation.

  - Add insulating materials like leaves, pine branches, or grass inside the shelter for added warmth.

TECHNIQUES FOR DIFFERENT WEATHER CONDITIONS:

Cold Weather:

- **Stay Dry:** Moisture reduces insulation; avoid sweating by regulating clothing layers.

- **Maintain Body Heat:** Wear a hat and layers, especially focusing on keeping your core warm.

- **Heat Source**: Build a fire and use rocks heated near the fire to retain warmth in the shelter.

Wet Weather:

- **Waterproofing**: Ensure your outer layer is waterproof to prevent rain from penetrating.

- **Dry Clothes**: Change into dry clothing as soon as possible if you get wet.

- **Elevated Sleeping Surface**: Raise your bedding above the ground in case of wet conditions.

Essential Tips:

- **Proper Sleeping Arrangements**:

  - Use insulating materials under your sleeping bag or mat to avoid losing body heat to the ground.

  - A reflective emergency blanket underneath can help reflect body heat back to you.

- **Stay Hydrated and Nourished:**

  - Hydration and nutrition are crucial for maintaining body temperature; eat and drink regularly.

- **Emergency Preparedness:**

  - Carry emergency heat sources like hand warmers or emergency blankets for immediate warmth.

  - Learn how to improvise emergency shelters using available materials if necessary.

Review and Refinement:

Learning from Experience:

- Reflect on your experiences in different weather conditions.

- Adapt and refine your techniques based on what worked best for staying warm and dry.

While this information provides guidance on staying warm and dry in various conditions, remember that individual situations may vary, and adaptation to specific environments is essential for a safe and comfortable wilderness experience.

WATER SOURCING AND PURIFICATION

Water Procurement in the Wilderness: Water, a vital component for survival, necessitates adept procurement techniques, particularly in remote areas. This chapter focuses on discovering and ensuring the safety of water sources in untamed terrains.

IMPORTANCE OF CLEAN WATER:

- **Essentiality:** Water is indispensable for all life forms, making its sourcing a fundamental survival skill.

- **Significance:** Securing access to uncontaminated potable water is crucial, especially in harsh environments.

IDENTIFYING WATER SOURCES:

- **Natural Sources**: Streams, rivers, and lakes are potential natural sources that can provide clean water after filtration.

  - *Observation:* Flourishing vegetation and wildlife presence often signify clean water in the vicinity.

- **Man-Made Alternatives**: Wells or rainwater collection systems offer reliable water sources.

  - *Accessibility:* Wells near populated areas can be accessed with basic tools like ropes and buckets.

  - *Rainwater Harvesting:* Collecting rainwater from rooftops requires more setup but can provide dependable water.

STRATEGIES FOR WATER SOURCING:

- **Human Activity Signs:** Trails or roads might lead to established water bodies like lakes or rivers.

- **Safety Assessment:** Ensuring safety before consumption is crucial through filtration and purification methods.

FILTRATION AND PURIFICATION TECHNIQUES:

- **Boiling:** Effective for killing pathogens and making water safe for consumption.

- **Chemical Treatment:** Using chemicals like chlorine or iodine tablets to purify water.

- **Filtration:** Utilizing filters to remove sediments, contaminants, and larger particles.

MASTERING WATER SOURCING:

- **Crucial Skill:** Learning to locate clean water sources is essential for survival in the wilderness.

- **Method Embrace:** By adopting these methodologies, children can effectively identify safe water sources, ensuring hydration and well-being.

Understanding these methodologies equips individuals, especially children, with essential skills to identify and ensure the safety of water sources in remote environments, fostering self-sufficiency and safety in the wilderness.

WATER PURIFICATION TECHNIQUES

Boiling Water:

Boiling water is a reliable method for water purification in the wilderness. By bringing collected water to a rolling boil for at least one minute, pathogens such as bacteria, viruses, and parasites are effectively killed. Boiling water doesn't require additional tools or chemicals and is highly effective.

Water Filtration:

Using water filters or purifiers is another effective method. These devices usually consist of a micron filter capable of straining out bacteria, protozoa, and sediment. Water filtration is convenient and maintains the taste of water, making it suitable for outdoor activities like camping.

Chemical Treatment:

Chemical treatments involving chlorine or iodine tablets/drops effectively disinfect water. Following the manufacturer's instructions regarding dosage and waiting time ensures the elimination of pathogens. These lightweight treatments are convenient for carrying in emergency kits.

UV Water Purification:

Utilizing UV water purifiers, which use ultraviolet light to deactivate pathogens, is a fast and effective method. It doesn't alter the taste of water and eliminates the need for chemicals or boiling when used correctly.

Solar Water Disinfection (SODIS):

SODIS utilizes sunlight to disinfect water in clear plastic bottles. Placing PET bottles filled with water in direct sunlight for at least 6 hours effectively disinfects the water. It's an eco-friendly and cost-effective method suitable for areas with limited resources.

Improvised Filtration:

In emergency situations, improvised filters using layers of cloth, sand, charcoal, or gravel can remove large particles and some microorganisms. While these methods might not offer the same level of purification as dedicated tools, they can be useful when conventional methods aren't available.

Importance of Water Purification

Mastering these techniques is crucial for ensuring access to safe drinking water in the wilderness. For children exploring remote terrains, these skills are invaluable, providing the means to identify and purify water sources. It not only guarantees hydration but also safeguards against waterborne illnesses, making them essential survival skills.

Conclusion

In the wilderness, accessing safe drinking water is paramount. Equipping children with the knowledge and proficiency to identify and purify water sources ensures their hydration and well-being despite challenging circumstances. Whether boiling water, using filters, or relying on UV light or chemical treatments, each method offers a reliable means to secure safe drinking water in untamed environments, fostering independence and safety for young adventurers exploring the wild.

COLLECTING RAINWATER OR DEW:

Gathering Rainwater:

- **Set Up for Rainwater Collection:**

    - Use a clean, wide container like a tarp or a large, clean bottle during rainfall.

    - Place the container in an open area away from trees to prevent debris from entering.

- **Rainwater Harvesting:**

- Utilize various containers like tarps, ponchos, or a tent rain fly.

- Ensure the collection surface is clean and free from contaminants.

- **Improvised Rainwater Collection:**

  - Create a makeshift gutter using leaves, branches, or other materials to direct rainwater into your collection container.

Harvesting Dew:

- **Dew Collection Techniques:**

  - Use absorbent materials like clean cloth or clothing to wipe dew from plants, grass, or surfaces early in the morning.

  - Wring out the cloth into a container to collect the dew.

- **Dew Gathering Cloth:**

  - Hang clean, absorbent fabric exposed to dew formation overnight.

- Squeeze out the collected moisture into a container.

CONSIDERATIONS FOR RAINWATER AND DEW COLLECTION:

Cleanliness and Storage:

- Ensure clean collection containers or materials to prevent contamination.

- Store collected rainwater or dew in tightly sealed containers to maintain cleanliness.

Quantity and Availability:

- Rainwater or dew collection may yield small quantities; consider multiple collection points or methods for a sufficient supply.

Safety and Treatment:

- Treat collected rainwater or dew using purification methods like boiling, filtration, or chemical treatment to eliminate potential contaminants.

Emergency And Supplemental Water Source:

Supplemental Water Supply:

- Rainwater or dew collection serves as an additional water source during dry spells or water scarcity.

- Use it as a supplement to other purification methods or available natural water sources.

Precautions:

Environmental Considerations:

- Collect rainwater or dew from clean surfaces to avoid contamination.

- Be cautious about using dew from areas where pesticides or chemicals might have been sprayed.

Storage and Consumption:

- Store collected rainwater or dew properly to prevent contamination.

- Treat the collected water before drinking to eliminate potential pathogens.

Collecting rainwater or dew can supplement your freshwater supply in the wilderness. However, ensure safety measures, treat the water, and maintain cleanliness to avoid potential contamination.

Finding Food in the Wild: A Guide to Foraging

UNDERSTANDING FORAGING BASICS

- **Necessity of Foraging:**

    - Foraging for food is a critical skill in the wild, providing sustenance when resources are scarce.

    - Proper knowledge prevents ingesting poisonous plants, ensuring safety.

- **Importance of Plant Identification:**

    - Vital survival skill to recognize edible plants and berries, enhancing food sources.

    - Prevents the consumption of toxic plants, ensuring safety during foraging.

BASICS OF PLANT IDENTIFICATION

- **Learning Plant Features:**

  - Gain knowledge from field guides, courses, or guided nature walks to identify plants.

  - Observe characteristics like leaves, stems, flowers, and growth patterns for accurate identification.

- **Common Edible Plants and Berries:**

  - Examples include dandelion, wild garlic, blueberries, blackberries, raspberries, and strawberries.

  - Recognizable features and distinct growth patterns aid in identification.

IDENTIFYING EDIBLE PLANTS

- **Visual Identification:**

- Pay attention to leaf shape, color, vein patterns, and distinct features for accurate identification.

- Use reliable field guides or online resources for cross-referencing and confirmation.

- **Smell and Touch:**

  - Some edible plants have unique smells or textures; rubbing leaves can release identifying scents.

  - Physical examination aids in distinguishing edible species.

- **Poisonous Plant Awareness:**

  - Recognize and avoid common poisonous plants like poison ivy, poison oak, or plants resembling them.

  - Cautionary identification to prevent accidental ingestion of toxic species.

FORAGING ETHICS AND SUSTAINABILITY

- **Responsible Foraging:**

    - Harvest plants in moderation, preserving the ecosystem and preventing over-harvesting.

    - Avoid unnecessary damage or uprooting of plants while foraging.

- **Leave No Trace Principles:**

    - Follow ethical practices by minimizing impact and maintaining the foraging area's natural state.

    - Uphold environmental conservation by leaving minimal to no evidence of foraging activities.

LEARNING AND PRECAUTIONS

- **Consulting Experts:**

- Seek advice from local botanists, foraging experts, or indigenous communities for accurate information.

- Gather insights from experienced individuals for practical guidance and better understanding.

- **Precautionary Measures:**

  - Exercise caution as some edible plants have poisonous look-alikes; accurate identification is essential.

  - Avoid plants near polluted areas or roadsides, ensuring foraged items are from safe environments.

Identifying edible plants and berries in the wilderness is a valuable skill, providing additional sustenance during outdoor expeditions. Caution, knowledge, and practice are key to safe and successful foraging.

IDENTIFYING COMMON EDIBLE PLANTS AND BERRIES

Dandelion (Taraxacum officinale)

- **Identification:**

    - *Leaves:* Deeply toothed, forming a rosette close to the ground.

    - *Flowers:* Bright yellow, single stem arising from the rosette.

- **Edibility:**

    - *Usage:* Leaves in salads, roots brewed as tea.

Wild Garlic (Allium vineale)

- **Identification:**

    - *Leaves:* Long, slender, emit a strong garlic smell when crushed.

    - *Bulbs:* Small bulbs resembling miniature garlic bulbs.

- **Edibility:**

    - *Usage:* Leaves in cooking, bulbs raw or cooked.

Wild Berries

- **Blueberries (Vaccinium spp.):**

  - *Identification:* Round, blue-purple berries on low shrubs in clusters.

  - *Edibility:* Safe and delicious eaten raw or used in recipes.

- **Blackberries (Rubus spp.):**

  - *Identification:* Dark-colored, plump berries on thorny canes.

  - *Edibility:* Edible when ripe, used in various culinary uses.

- **Raspberries (Rubus idaeus):**

  - *Identification:* Red, pink, or black berries on thorny canes.

  - *Edibility:* Sweet and used fresh or in desserts.

- **Strawberries (Fragaria spp.):**

  - *Identification:* Small, red berries with seeds on the surface.

- *Edibility:* Eaten fresh or in various dishes.

Lamb's Quarters (Chenopodium album)

- **Identification:**
    - *Leaves:* Goose foot-shaped, toothed edges, powdery underside.
    - *Stems:* Reddish, branching with small green flowers.
- **Edibility:**
    - *Usage:* Young leaves in salads or cooked dishes.

Plantain (Plantago major)

- **Identification:**
    - *Leaves:* Broad, oval, prominent parallel veins.
    - *Flowers:* Small, greenish-white on tall stalks.
- **Edibility:**

- *Usage:* Young leaves cooked in soups or as a green vegetable.

Common Purslane (Portulaca oleracea)

- **Identification:**

    - *Leaves:* Succulent, smooth, spoon-shaped, reddish stems.

    - *Stems:* Thick, reddish, sprawling.

- **Edibility:**

    - *Usage:* Eaten raw in salads or cooked as a vegetable.

Elderberry (Sambucus spp.)

- **Identification:**

    - *Berries:* Small, dark purple to black in umbrella-shaped clusters.

    - *Leaves:* Opposite, compound with toothed edges.

- **Edibility:**

    - *Usage:* Berries cooked in various recipes.

Wild Strawberries (Fragaria vesca)

- **Identification:**

  - *Berries:* Smaller, intense flavor, red to dark red.

  - *Leaves:* Compound with three toothed leaflets.

- **Edibility:**

  - *Usage:* Similar to cultivated strawberries, eaten fresh in dishes.

IDENTIFYING EDIBLE ANIMALS IN THE WILDERNESS

Recognizing safe-to-consume animals is crucial for wilderness survival. Consider these essential tips:

Area Familiarity

- **Research the Region:** Learn about the animals commonly found in the area where you'll be camping. Familiarity aids in identifying potential edible options.

- **Local Species:** Recognize prevalent species and understand their characteristics to discern which are safe for consumption.

Observe Local Practices

- **Learn from Locals:** Observe local inhabitants' hunting practices and their choice of edible animals. This offers valuable insights into safe options and preparation methods.

Species Research

- **Understand Local Fauna:** Delve into the diverse species inhabiting the area. Knowledge about the local wildlife helps in distinguishing edible creatures from non-edible ones.

Utilize Your Senses

- **Observation:** Engage your senses – sight, hearing, and smell. Look for signs of animal presence like tracks, fur, or droppings. Listen for rustling or calls. Detect animal scents using your sense of smell.

Assess Edibility Signs

Health Indicators: Evaluate indicators of an animal's edibility, such as healthy fur, adequate fat reserves, and overall physical condition. Avoid animals that appear sickly or emaciated.

BASIC TRAP TECHNIQUES FOR WILDERNESS SURVIVAL

Deadfall Trap

Materials Needed:

- Heavy object (rock or log) for the deadfall.
- Three sticks: one for the base, one for the diagonal support, and one for the trigger stick.
- Cordage or natural fibers for tying.

Steps to Build:

- Find a heavy object suitable as the deadfall weight.
- Create an "L" shaped base stick on the ground.
- Position the diagonal support stick against the base stick, leaning on the heavy object.
- Lay the trigger stick across the top of the diagonal stick, touching the base stick slightly.
- Tie the trigger stick to the diagonal stick, allowing it to pivot freely.
- Place bait under the heavy object. When disturbed, the trigger stick releases, causing the deadfall to trap the prey.

Hand Line Fishing

Equipment Needed:

- Fishing line (durable and strong).
- Fishing hook(s) of various sizes.
- Bait (worms, insects, or small fish pieces).

Technique: Setup:

- Attach the hook securely to the fishing line.
- Securely attach the bait to the hook.

Casting and Retrieval:

- Stand near the water's edge or on a pier.
- Cast the line into the water, allowing it to sink to a desired depth.
- Patiently wait for a fish to bite.
- When a fish bites, jerk or reel in the line swiftly to hook the fish.
- Gradually reel in the catch, keeping tension on the line.

Maintenance:

Regularly check the bait and adjust the depth or location of the line to attract fish.

Snare Trap

Materials Needed:

- Sturdy cordage, wire, or natural fibers.
- A small, flexible sapling or branch for the loop.

Steps to Build:

- Form a small, strong yet flexible noose using the cordage.
- Create a loop by tying a secure knot on one end of the cordage.
- Anchor the looped end to a stable object or stake in the ground.
- Place the snare in areas frequented by animals or near burrows to trigger the loop around the prey's neck or body.

Precautions:

- Regularly check the snare to prevent unintended captures or undue suffering to animals.
- Adhere to local laws and ethical guidelines regarding the use of snare traps.

Figure-4 Deadfall Trap

Materials:

- Three sticks of similar length: for base, diagonal support, and trigger stick.
- Cordage or natural fibers for securing.

Steps to Build:

- Create an "L" shape with the base stick on the ground.
- Place the diagonal support stick against the base stick at an angle.
- Position the trigger stick horizontally on top of the diagonal stick, slightly touching the base stick.
- Tie the trigger stick to the diagonal stick, allowing it to pivot freely.
- Set bait under the structure. When triggered, the trap falls, capturing the prey.

Caution:

- Set the trap carefully to prevent accidental triggering or injury.

- Regularly check the trap to avoid unintended catches.

Fish Trap

Materials:

- Basket, mesh, or netting material.
- Sticks or supports to frame the trap.
- Bait (fish scraps, insects, or attractants).

Steps to Build:

- Construct a frame using sticks or supports.
- Weave or attach the basket, mesh, or netting, leaving an entry point for fish.
- Place bait inside and position the trap in shallow waters or fish migration paths.

Retrieving Catch:

- Check the trap periodically to retrieve captured fish.
- Avoid leaving fish in the trap for too long to prevent spoilage or escape.

Spear Fishing

Equipment and Technique:

- Long, sturdy stick or branch with a sharpened tip.
- Alternatively, create a multi-pronged spear by splitting and sharpening the stick.

Fishing Technique:

- Stand in shallow waters or fish-congregating areas.
- Aim the spear at fish within striking range.
- Thrust the spear quickly and accurately to impale the fish.

Caution and Preparation:

- Handle the sharp-tipped spear cautiously to prevent injury.
- Practice aiming and striking fish accurately and quietly.

HUNTING WITH A BOW OR SLINGSHOT

HUNTING WITH A BOW

Equipment and Preparation:

Bow Components: Choose from recurve, longbow, or compound bow.

Arrows: Use durable arrows with sharp broadheads for hunting.

Skill and Technique:

Practice: Regularly practice archery to develop accuracy and aiming skills.

Technique: Familiarize yourself with the bow's draw weight and aiming for different distances.

Hunting Technique:

Stealth and Patience: Move quietly and choose hunting spots with cover.

Aiming and Shooting: Aim for vital areas on the animal and wait for the right moment to shoot.

Recovery and Follow-Up:

After the Shot: Give the animal time to expire before tracking it.

Tracking: Follow the blood trail or signs of the animal's movement to recover the game.

HUNTING WITH A SLINGSHOT

Equipment and Preparation:

Slingshot Components: Choose a durable slingshot with quality bands and a comfortable grip.

Ammunition: Utilize steel or lead pellets, marbles, or small rocks as ammunition.

Accuracy and Practice:

Regular Practice: Enhance accuracy and proficiency by consistently aiming and shooting at targets.

Ammo Experimentation: Experiment with various ammunition types to understand their trajectory and impact.

Hunting Technique:

Stealth and Positioning: Approach hunting spots quietly and conceal yourself using natural cover or camouflage.

Aiming and Shot Placement: Aim for vital areas for an effective kill shot and wait for the right moment to take a precise shot.

ETHICAL CONSIDERATIONS:

Accuracy and Humanity: Ensure accurate shots to minimize animal suffering and aim for a humane kill.

Confident Shots: Only take shots when confident of a swift and humane outcome.

Safety and Legal Considerations:

Safety Precautions: Prioritize safety by employing proper handling techniques and adhering to safety guidelines.

Adherence to Laws: Follow local hunting laws, including regulations on permitted species, hunting seasons, and mandatory licenses.

Hunting using a slingshot demands skill, practice, and ethical responsibility. Ensure safety, adhere to legal regulations, and exercise respect and humane consideration toward wildlife while employing this method for survival.

BOW HUNTING - AIMING AND SHOOTING TECHNIQUE:

I. AIMING TECHNIQUES:

Anchor Point:

- **Consistent Anchor:** Maintain a steady anchor point (e.g., corner of the mouth or chin) when drawing the bowstring for consistent and accurate shots.

- **Reference Point:** It serves as a consistent reference for aiming, ensuring uniformity in shots.

Sight Alignment:

- **Utilizing Aiming Aids**: Align the bow sight or use the arrow's tip as an aiming reference.

- **Focused Aim**: Concentrate on the target while keeping the sight aligned for improved accuracy.

2. SHOOTING TECHNIQUE:

Release:

- **Smooth Release**: Execute a controlled and smooth release of the bowstring to avoid any abrupt changes in the arrow's flight path.

- **Minimize Disruption**: Jerky movements during release can significantly affect arrow trajectory.

Follow-Through:

- **Post-Shot Position**: Maintain your shooting stance and aim position even after releasing the arrow.

- **Consistent Form**: Helps in evaluating shot accuracy and ensures consistent shooting form.

SLINGSHOT HUNTING - AIMING AND SHOT PLACEMENT:

1. AIMING TECHNIQUES:

Point of Aim:

- **Specific Target**: Focus on a precise spot on the target to achieve accurate aiming.

- **Adjust for Distance**: Account for the slingshot's projectile trajectory concerning the target's distance.

Consistent Pull:

- **Uniform Anchor Point**: Pull the slingshot bands back consistently to the same anchor point for each shot.

- **Aid to Accuracy**: Ensures control and enhances the shot's precision.

2. SHOT PLACEMENT:

Critical Areas:

- **Vital Target Spots:** Aim for crucial areas like the head or chest for an effective and ethical shot.

- **Accuracy Importance:** Precision targeting in these areas is key for a swift and humane kill.

Safety Reminders:

- **Safety Gear:** Always use necessary protective gear suitable for the hunting method, like arm guards for bow hunting and eye protection for slingshots.

Skill Development:

- **Regular Practice:** Consistently practice aiming, shot placement, and safety measures in controlled settings to refine hunting skills.

- **Tool Familiarization:** Get acquainted with the handling and maintenance specifics of your chosen hunting tool to optimize its performance.

Mastering these specific techniques, including aiming, shot placement, and safety practices, is fundamental for successful hunting with a bow or a slingshot, ensuring accuracy, ethical hunting, and safety.

Food Preservation Techniques in the Wilderness

DRYING:

Air Drying:

- **Hanging Method:** Hang thinly sliced meat, fruits, or herbs in well-ventilated areas to facilitate air drying.

- **Thin Spread:** Ensure food is spread thinly for faster and effective drying by reducing moisture content.

Sun Drying:

- **Direct Sunlight:** Place food items on a clean surface exposed to direct sunlight to dehydrate naturally.

- **Rotation:** Rotate the food occasionally to ensure uniform drying on all sides.

SMOKING:

Smoking Process:

- **Smokehouse or Make-shift Smoker:** Construct a smoker or use a fire with a drying rack above it.

- **Exposure to Smoke:** Smoke acts as a preservative; expose meat or fish to the smoke for preservation.

CURING:

Salt Curing:

- **Salt Layer:** Cover meat or fish with salt to extract moisture and prevent bacterial growth.

- **Storage:** Keep the salted food in a cool, dry place for preservation.

Brine Solution:

- **Saltwater Mixture:** Submerge food in a saltwater solution, adding spices or herbs for enhanced flavor.

- **Preservation:** The brine solution aids in preservation.

FERMENTATION:

Lactic Acid Fermentation:

- **Saltwater Solution**: Submerge vegetables in saltwater or pack them in a container for natural fermentation.

- **Preservation and Flavor**: Fermentation preserves the food while enhancing its flavor.

ROOT CELLARING:

Underground Storage:

- **Natural Refrigeration**: Bury root vegetables like carrots or potatoes underground for a cool storage option.

- **Location Choice**: Opt for stable temperature spots with adequate insulation.

PICKLING:

Vinegar Pickling:

- **Vinegar Submersion**: Submerge fruits or vegetables in vinegar to create a pickling solution.

- **Preservative Acidity:** The acidic environment inhibits bacterial growth, extending the shelf life.

STORAGE IN NATURAL CONDITIONS:

Cooling by Water Bodies:

- **Submerged Storage:** Seal perishable foods in containers and immerse them in cool water to maintain freshness.

- **Regular Change:** Change the water periodically to ensure cleanliness and continued cooling.

Proper Packaging:

Sealing and Protection:

- **Airtight Containers:** Use sealable bags or airtight containers to protect food from moisture and pests.

- **Additional Protection:** Wrap food securely in leaves or cloth for added protection.

IMPORTANT CONSIDERATIONS:

- **Regular Monitoring**: Monitor food preservation processes frequently to ensure effectiveness and safety.

- **Clean Storage**: Keep food storage areas clean and free from contaminants to avoid spoilage.

- **Labeling and Monitoring**: Label preserved items, monitor expiration dates, and observe their effectiveness over time for safety and quality.

Mastering these food preservation techniques in the wilderness is crucial for self-sufficiency during extended stays, ensuring a sustainable and diverse food supply.

TOOLS FOR EASY FORAGING

Maps

Maps are essential aids for foragers, aiding in navigation and identifying locations of edible plants and resources. They help mark potential foraging areas, enabling easier retracing of steps and planning future expeditions.

Journals

Journals serve as valuable companions, allowing children to document environmental observations. They aid in recording found resources, their locations, and time of discovery, promoting a deeper understanding of the surroundings.

Field Guides

Field guides offer detailed insights into plant and animal identification. They provide essential information on environmental conditions conducive to specific species, assisting in determining the best time and place for foraging. F oraging is made easier with tools like maps, journals, and field guides, enhancing understanding and ensuring safe, responsible, and sustainable foraging practices.

Wilderness First Aid: Dealing With Cuts, Scrapes, and Minor Injuries

When navigating the wilderness, knowing how to manage cuts, scrapes, and minor injuries is crucial for ensuring safety and preventing infections. Here are comprehensive steps for handling such situations:

1. Assessing the Injury:

Wound Evaluation:

- Inspect the wound for size, depth, and foreign objects.

- Use clean hands or gloves to avoid introducing bacteria.

Bleeding Control:

- Apply firm, direct pressure using clean cloth or gauze to stop bleeding.

- Elevate the injured area above heart level to reduce blood flow.

2. Cleaning and Sanitization:

Thorough Cleaning:

- Rinse the wound with clean water to remove debris.

- Avoid using soap directly on the wound.

Antiseptic Application:

- Apply antiseptic solution or wipes around the wound to reduce infection risk.

- Avoid direct contact of iodine or alcohol-based solutions with the wound.

3. Dressing the Wound:

Proper Dressing:

- Apply antibiotic ointment to aid healing and prevent infection.

- Cover the wound with a sterile, non-adherent dressing.

Secure Bandaging:

- Use medical tape or adhesive bandages to secure the dressing without restricting blood flow.

4. Bandaging and Protection:

Change Dressings Regularly:

- Monitor the wound for signs of infection and change dressings as needed.

- Keep the wound area clean and dry to promote healing.

Use of Butterfly Bandages:

- Apply butterfly bandages for smaller cuts to hold wound edges together.

5. Monitoring and Follow-Up:

Observation:

- Check the wound daily for signs of infection such as redness, swelling, warmth, or discharge.

- Seek medical attention if the wound shows signs of infection or doesn't heal properly.

6. Wilderness First Aid Kit Essentials:

Essential Supplies:

- Ensure your kit has bandages, gauze pads, antiseptic wipes, adhesive tape, scissors, and tweezers.

- Include a CPR mask, pain relievers, and personal medications if required.

7. Additional Tips:

Preventing Further Injury:

- Avoid activities that may reopen or irritate the wound.

- Shield the wound from sun exposure and dirt to minimize infection risks.

Rest and Recovery:

- Encourage rest and elevate the injured area to reduce swelling and aid healing

Understanding and addressing common outdoor ailments is pivotal for ensuring safety and well-being in the wilderness. Here's an extensive guide covering various outdoor ailments and their treatments:

1. Sunburn:

Prevention:

- Use high SPF sunscreen and reapply regularly.
- Wear protective clothing and seek shade during peak sun hours.

Treatment:

- Apply aloe vera or a cool compress to soothe the affected area.
- Take over-the-counter pain relievers like ibuprofen for discomfort.
- Drink plenty of water to stay hydrated.

2. Insect Bites and Stings:

Prevention:

- Use insect repellent and wear protective clothing.

- Avoid perfumes or scented products that attract insects.

Treatment:

- Remove the stinger if present by scraping it away with a credit card.

- Apply a cold compress or hydrocortisone cream to reduce swelling and itching.

- Monitor for signs of allergic reactions and seek medical help if severe.

3. Poisonous Plant Exposure:

Prevention:

- Learn to identify poisonous plants and avoid contact.

- Wear long clothing and gloves when hiking in areas known for poisonous plants.

Treatment:

- Wash the affected area with soap and water immediately.

- Apply a cold compress and take antihistamines for itching.

- Seek medical help if experiencing severe reactions or difficulty breathing.

4. Dehydration:

Prevention:

- Drink plenty of water throughout the day, even if not thirsty.

- Consume electrolyte-rich drinks or carry rehydration salts.

Treatment:

- Rest in a shaded area and slowly drink water or rehydration fluids.

- Avoid caffeine or alcohol, which can worsen dehydration.

- Seek medical attention if symptoms persist or worsen.

5. Heat Exhaustion:

Prevention:

- Stay hydrated and take breaks in shaded or cool areas.

- Wear light-colored, loose-fitting clothing.

Treatment:

- Move to a cooler place and rest.

- Apply cool, wet cloths to the body or take a cool shower.

- Seek medical help if experiencing confusion, fainting, or vomiting.

6. Hypothermia:

Prevention:

- Dress in layers and stay dry in cold conditions.

- Keep moving to generate body heat.

Treatment:

- Get to a warm, dry area and change into dry clothes.

- Use blankets or sleeping bags to increase body heat.

- Seek immediate medical attention if severe symptoms are present.

7. Blisters:

Prevention:

- Wear properly fitting footwear and moisture-wicking socks.

- Use blister-prevention products or tape vulnerable areas.

Treatment:

- Keep the blister clean and intact if possible to prevent infection.

- Apply a blister pad or moleskin to relieve pressure.

- If the blister breaks, clean the area and apply an antibiotic ointment.

8. Sprains and Strains:

Prevention:

- Warm up before physical activities and use proper gear.

- Avoid overexertion and be mindful of your movements.

Treatment:

- Rest the affected area and apply ice wrapped in a cloth for 15-20 minutes every few hours.

- Compress the area with a bandage to reduce swelling.

- Elevate the injured area to minimize swelling.

9. Diarrhea:

Prevention:

- Drink clean, purified water and eat properly cooked food.

- Practice good hand hygiene before eating.

Treatment:

- Stay hydrated by drinking plenty of clean water or oral rehydration solutions.

- Avoid spicy, fatty, or hard-to-digest foods until symptoms subside.

- Seek medical help if diarrhea persists or is severe.

10. Altitude Sickness:

Prevention:

- Ascend gradually to higher altitudes to acclimatize.

- Stay hydrated and avoid excessive physical exertion.

Treatment:

- Descend to a lower altitude if symptoms worsen.

- Rest and hydrate adequately.

- Medications like acetazolamide can help prevent or alleviate symptoms.

11. Tick Bites:

Prevention:

- Wear long sleeves and pants in wooded or grassy areas.

- Use insect repellent containing DEET or permethrin.

Treatment:

- Remove the tick with fine-tipped tweezers, grasping it as close to the skin's surface as possible and pulling upward steadily.

- Clean the bite area with soap and water and apply an antiseptic.

- Monitor for signs of Lyme disease or other tick-borne illnesses.

12. Snake Bites:

Prevention:

- Be aware of surroundings and avoid stepping on or near places where snakes may hide.

- Wear protective footwear and clothing in snake-prone areas.

Treatment:

- Keep the bitten area immobilized and below heart level.

- Seek immediate medical attention.

- Do not attempt to suck out venom or use a tourniquet.

COMMON PLANTS AND THEIR USES IN NATURAL REMEDIES:

1. Aloe Vera:

Uses:

- **Sunburn Relief**: Apply the gel directly from the aloe vera leaves onto sunburnt skin to soothe and cool the affected area.

- **Minor Burns**: Aloe vera gel may help alleviate pain and promote healing for minor burns.

2. Lavender:

Uses:

- **Calming Properties**: Lavender oil or dried lavender flowers can be used in aromatherapy to reduce stress, anxiety, and promote relaxation.

- **Antiseptic**: Lavender oil possesses mild antiseptic properties. Diluted oil can be applied to minor cuts and wounds.

3. Peppermint:

Uses:

- **Digestive Aid**: Peppermint tea made from leaves may help alleviate symptoms of indigestion, gas, and nausea.

- **Cooling Effect**: Crushed mint leaves can be rubbed onto the skin to provide a cooling sensation and relieve minor itching.

4. Chamomile:

Uses:

- **Skin Irritations**: Chamomile tea or poultice made from flowers may calm skin irritations, minor rashes, and insect bites.

- **Relaxation**: Drinking chamomile tea can promote relaxation and aid in better sleep.

5. Echinacea:

Uses:

- **Immune Support**: Echinacea tea made from its roots or flowers might help support the immune system, potentially aiding in fighting minor infections like colds.

- **Antibacterial**: It may have antibacterial properties useful in preventing minor infections.

6. Garlic:

Uses:

- **Antibacterial**: Crushed garlic can be applied to minor wounds for its potential antibacterial effects.

- **Immune Support**: Consumption of garlic may help in supporting the immune system.

7. Willow Bark:

Uses:

- **Pain Relief**: Willow bark contains salicin, a compound similar to aspirin, which can provide pain relief for minor headaches and injuries.

- **Anti-inflammatory**: It may reduce inflammation in minor injuries or pains.

8. Yarrow:

Uses:

- **Wound Healing**: Yarrow poultices or crushed leaves may help stop bleeding and promote healing in minor cuts and wounds.

- **Anti-inflammatory**: Topical application might help reduce inflammation in minor skin irritations.

9. Plantain:

Uses:

- **Skin Healing**: Plantain leaves can be applied as a poultice to relieve insect stings, bites, or minor cuts due to their potential anti-inflammatory properties.

- **Antimicrobial**: It might help in preventing minor wound infections.

Safety Note:

- Correct identification of plants is crucial before using them. Misidentification can lead to using toxic plants.

- Be cautious about allergic reactions. Test a small area before applying a plant-based remedy extensively.

Always consult with a healthcare professional or herbalist before using natural remedies, especially in severe cases or if you have allergies or pre-existing conditions. They can provide personalized advice based on individual health considerations.

ELABORATION ON RECOGNIZING AND TREATING SNAKE BITES OR INSECT STINGS IN THE WILDERNESS:

1. Snake Bites:

Recognition:

- **Two Puncture Marks:** Most venomous snake bites leave two puncture marks on the skin.

- **Swelling and Pain:** Swelling, redness, and severe pain around the bite area are common symptoms.

- **Nausea, Dizziness, Weakness:** These symptoms may appear if the snake is venomous.

Treatment:

- **Stay Calm:** Keep the bitten area below heart level to slow venom spread.

- **Remove Jewelry or Tight Clothing:** Swelling might occur.

- **Clean the Bite Area:** Wash with soap and water.

- **Apply a Bandage:** Use a clean, dry bandage to cover the bite area with firm pressure but not tight to impede blood flow.

- **Seek Medical Help:** Get to a hospital or call emergency services immediately.

Do NOT:

- **Apply a tourniquet or ice.**

- **Cut the wound or attempt to suck out venom.**

- Use a constricting bandage unless advised by medical personnel.

2. Insect Stings:

Recognition:

- **Localized Pain and Swelling**: Immediate pain and swelling at the sting site.

- **Redness and Itching**: The affected area might turn red and itch intensely.

Treatment:

- **Remove Stinger**: Scrape the stinger out sideways with a fingernail or blunt object to avoid squeezing more venom into the skin.

- **Clean the Area**: Wash with soap and water.

- **Apply a Cold Compress**: Helps reduce swelling and ease pain.

- **Use Over-the-counter Remedies**: Antihistamines or hydrocortisone cream can alleviate itching and swelling.

- **Seek Medical Help if**: The person stung experiences severe allergic reactions, difficulty breathing, or if multiple stings occur.

Do NOT:

- **Scratch the area vigorously, as it can lead to further irritation and potential infection.**

- **Apply vinegar, urine, or other unconventional remedies, which might worsen the situation.**

Recognizing the symptoms of snake bites and insect stings is crucial for prompt and appropriate action. Immediate treatment involves cleaning the affected area and seeking medical attention, especially in severe cases or when dealing with venomous snakes.

Creating Fire in the Wild: Techniques Explored

The art of igniting fires in the wilderness is an intriguing journey, brimming with essential knowledge. This section delves into the core principles of fire-making, offering diverse methodologies for mastering this fundamental skill. By the chapter's close, a comprehensive understanding of fire ignition ensures the ability to safely and effectively kindle fires amidst nature's grandeur. Let's explore the basics!

GATHERING FIREWOOD

Proficiency in sourcing firewood from nature is a crucial skill, especially for young adventurers exploring the outdoors. It ensures warmth and security during expeditions.

Step 1: Identifying the Ideal Source

Commence by locating optimal firewood sources. Dead or fallen trees and branches serve as prime candidates. It's pivotal to ensure the wood is dry rather than green, as green wood poses challenges in burning and tends to generate excessive smoke.

Step 2: Wood Collection

Once a suitable source is found, the next step involves gathering the wood. Use tools like a saw or axe to cut the wood into manageable pieces, prioritizing safety by using protective gear.

Step 3: Transporting Wood

After amassing enough firewood, focus on transporting it back to the campsite. Employ a wheelbarrow or sled and carry the wood with both hands for ease and safety during transportation.

Step 4: Firewood Preparation

Before starting the fire, proper preparation of the firewood is vital. Split the logs into smaller segments and create kindling using a knife or axe. These steps facilitate a swift and efficient ignition process.

PREPARING THE FIRE PIT

Step 1: Locating the Suitable Spot

Select an area away from trees, overhanging branches, and flammable materials like dry leaves. Ensure adequate drainage to prevent flooding during rain.

Step 2: Clearing the Designated Area

Clear the area by removing rocks, sticks, and debris that could ignite. Excavate the ground to create an 8-inch 'fire bed' to contain the fire safely.

Step 3: Procuring Rocks

Gather sizable rocks to encircle the fire pit, acting as a barrier to contain the flames. Collect rocks of similar size to create a secure boundary.

Step 4: Constructing the Fire Pit

Arrange the rocks in a circular formation around the fire bed, leaving an open space in the middle for the fire. Ensure the rocks are securely positioned without gaps for safe and contained burning.

INITIATING THE FIRE:

Essential Materials:

Before starting a fire in the wild, gather these crucial materials:

1. **Fire Pit Preparation**:

   - Dig a pit in the ground, roughly three feet in circumference, lining it with rocks for safety.

2. **Fire Starters**:

   - **Tinder**: Easily combustible material that catches a spark.

   - **Kindling**: Slightly larger wood pieces that help sustain the fire.

   - **Fuel**: Larger wood segments to prolong the fire's duration.

3. **Matches or Lighter**: Essential tools for igniting the fire.

Ignition Process:

1. **Arranging Materials**:

   - Place the tinder at the fire pit center. Surround it with kindling arranged in a tepee-like structure. Add fuel while ensuring it doesn't directly touch the tinder or kindling.

2. **Ignition**:

   - Use matches or a lighter to ignite the tinder. Blow gently to encourage combustion, allowing the fire to spread from tinder to kindling.

3. **Sustaining the Fire**:

   - As the kindling ignites, introduce larger fuel pieces gradually to sustain the fire.

USING FLINT, FRICTION, AND OTHER METHODS:

1. FLINT AND STEEL:

- **Materials Needed**: Flint/quartz rock and high-carbon steel striker/knife.

- **Procedure**: Strike the steel against the flint, directing sparks onto dry tinder to catch and encourage combustion.

2. FRICTION METHODS:

- Bow Drill:

  - **Materials Needed**: Bow, spindle, fire board, and socket.

  - **Procedure**: Rotate the spindle against a fire board using a bow to create friction, generating an ember to ignite tinder.

- Hand Drill:

  - **Materials Needed**: Fire board, spindle, and handhold.

139

- **Procedure**: Rub the spindle against a fire board using a handhold to create friction and produce an ember to ignite tinder.

3. OTHER METHODS:

- **Solar Ignition**: Utilize a magnifying glass or other reflective surface to focus sunlight onto tinder.

- **Chemical Reaction**: Use specific chemicals or a battery and steel wool to initiate a fire.

SAFETY TIPS FOR STARTING FIRES:

- **Prepare the Site**: Clear the fire pit area of flammable materials.

- **Adequate Tinder and Kindling**: Gather dry and fine materials for successful ignition.

- **Patience and Practice**: Practice these methods in a safe environment beforehand.

- **Complete Extinguishment**: After use, ensure the fire is entirely extinguished by dousing it with water and stirring the ashes.

Conclusion:

Mastering fire-starting methods in the wild is essential for survival. Practice these techniques and follow safety protocols for safe and successful fire ignition.

ENHANCING WILDERNESS FIRE-STARTING SKILLS

1. Material Preparation:

- **Tinder Variety**:

  - Gather diverse tinder types like dry grass, shredded bark, and cotton balls with petroleum jelly. Having varied options increases success chances.

- **Kindling Collection**:

- Collect small, dry sticks and twigs of different thicknesses to gradually sustain the fire.

2. **Technique Refinement:**

  - **Consistent Pressure**:

    - Maintain steady pressure and speed in friction-based methods (e.g., bow drill) to generate necessary heat and friction for ember creation.

  - **Angle Adjustment**:

    - Adjust the angle of the striking tool with flint and steel to direct sparks accurately onto the tinder bundle.

  - **Proper Alignment**:

    - Ensure stable material alignment to avoid unnecessary movement and energy loss.

3. **Fire Lay Preparation:**

  - **Use of Fire Lay**:

- Choose from teepee, log cabin, or lean-to structures based on available materials and weather conditions.

- **Ventilation**:

  - Arrange kindling to encourage airflow, vital for fire growth and sustenance.

4. Persistence and Patience:

- **Regular Practice**:

  - Practice in varied conditions (dry, windy, damp) to boost adaptability and proficiency.

- **Exercise Patience**:

  - Understand primitive methods might take time. Execute each step with patience and diligence.

5. **Safety Measures**:

- **Watch for Sparks**:

  - Be cautious of sparks while using flint or similar sparking methods. Ensure they don't accidentally ignite surrounding materials or clothing.

- **Fire Extinguishing**:

  - Keep water or fire extinguishing tools nearby. After use, completely extinguish the fire to prevent unintentional spreading.

- **Environmental Concerns**:

  - Adhere to leave-no-trace principles and confirm fires are permitted in the area.

Conclusion:

Enhancing fire-starting skills involves preparedness, technique refinement, and safety consciousness. Regular practice and familiarity with various methods significantly contribute to wilderness survival.

STRATEGIES FOR MAINTAINING FIRE IN ADVERSE CONDITIONS

WET CONDITIONS:

- **Dry Fuel Scarcity**: Rain and dampness make finding dry fuel challenging.

- **Water Ingress**: Moisture affects fire-starting materials, hindering ignition.

WINDY CONDITIONS:

- **Oxygen Depletion**: Strong winds deplete oxygen, challenging fire sustainability.

- **Fuel Consumption**: Wind disperses heat and consumes fuel faster.

PREPARING FOR ADVERSE CONDITIONS

Location Selection:

- **Sheltered Spots**: Choose areas shielded from winds like rock formations or dense trees.

145

- **Dry Ground**: Opt for elevated, dry ground to prevent water pooling around the fire pit.

Fuel Collection and Storage:

- **Elevated Sources**: Seek dry wood in standing deadwood or branches above ground.

- **Sheltered Storage**: Store collected dry fuel under tarps or in backpacks to shield from moisture.

FIRE-LAYING TECHNIQUES

Teepee Fire Lay:

- Construct a teepee structure with dry kindling in the center, gradually adding larger pieces for airflow.

Lean-to Fire Lay:

- Lean dry kindling against a log or rock to create a windbreak and focused flame.

Upside-down Fire Lay:

- Stack larger logs at the base, progressively smaller atop. Burns top-down, resisting dampness while allowing airflow.

TECHNIQUES FOR FIRE IGNITION

Use of Fire Starters:

- Employ dryer lint soaked in wax, alcohol-based hand sanitizers, or commercial fire starters to overcome dampness.

Char Cloth or Feathersticks:

- Use char cloth or feathersticks as highly flammable kindling options.

Fire Reflectors:

- Build a reflector wall with rocks or logs to redirect heat towards the fire and protect from wind.

ADDITIONAL TIPS:

- **Cover Firewood:** Covering firewood with a tarp or plastic sheeting helps prevent moisture absorption.

- **Keep Fuel Dry:** Keep a supply of dry fuel close to the fire to ensure a consistent burn.

- **Constant Monitoring:** Regularly tend to the fire, adding fuel as needed, and maintain fire reflectors for optimal heat redirection.

Successfully maintaining a fire in adverse conditions demands strategic fuel collection, placement, and ignition techniques. It's crucial to adapt methods to suit specific environmental challenges for effective fire sustainability.

FIRE MANAGEMENT STRATEGIES

GRADUAL FUEL ADDITION

- **Progressive Approach:** Add fuel incrementally, starting with smaller pieces, gradually adding larger logs as the fire grows.

MAINTAINING A BED OF COALS

- **Steady Heat Source**: Focus on preserving a bed of hot coals as they generate consistent heat, crucial in adverse conditions.

COVERING THE FIRE

- **Protection from Elements**: Shield the fire from rain or snow by placing a larger log or rock over it, allowing incoming fuel to dry.

CONTINUOUS FIRE TENDING

- **Constant Vigilance**: Maintain regular supervision of the fire to prevent unintentional extinguishing or spreading.

- **Fuel Gathering**: Continuously scout for additional fuel to sustain a steady fire.

- **Protection from Precipitation**: Employ a tarp or natural materials to protect the fire during persistent rainfall.

COOKING FOOD OVER A FIRE

ESSENTIAL COOKING EQUIPMENT

Cooking Vessels:

- *Camping Cookware:* Lightweight, durable pots, pans, and kettles suitable for outdoor cooking.

- *Skewers or Grates:* Ideal for grilling meats, vegetables, or fish over the flames.

Utensils:

- *Long-Handled Tongs or Forks:* Essential for handling food safely over the fire.

- *Sturdy Spatula:* Useful for flipping food or handling delicate items.

BASIC COOKING METHODS

Direct Flame Cooking:

- *Grilling:* Directly place food on skewers or grates for quick and flavorful cooking.

- *Roasting:* Skewer meats or vegetables and cook them over the fire until done.

Indirect Heat Cooking:

- *Campfire Stove:* Create a simple stove with rocks or logs to support pots or pans slightly above the flames for controlled cooking.

PREPARING FOOD FOR COOKING

Food Preparation:

- *Food Packing:* Store ingredients in sealable bags or containers to maintain freshness and prevent contamination.

- *Cutting and Slicing:* Prepare ingredients into smaller portions for faster, even cooking.

SEASONING AND FLAVORING:

- *Portable Spice Kit:* Carry essential spices in small containers to enhance meal flavors.

- *Marinades or Rubs:* Use flavorful marinades or spice rubs for meats and vegetables.

Conclusion

Surviving in challenging weather conditions requires adaptability and attention to the fire. Employing proper site selection, fuel preparation, fire-laying techniques, and continuous tending is crucial for sustaining fires in the wilderness. Moreover, mastering various cooking methods over an open fire enhances the culinary experience, providing nourishment and comfort during outdoor expeditions.

TECHNIQUES FOR COOKING DIFFERENT FOODS

MEATS

- **Steaks and Chops:** Grill directly over flames, adjusting height for preferred cooking levels.

- **Skewered Meats:** Thread meat chunks onto skewers, rotating for even cooking.

VEGETABLES

- **Foil Packets:** Seasoned vegetables in foil cooked on coals or near the fire for roasting.

- **Skewered Vegetables:** Alternate vegetable chunks on skewers and grill for a smoky flavor.

FISH

- **Foil-Wrapped Fish:** Season whole fish, wrap in foil with herbs/vegetables, and cook over flames.

- **Grilling on Grates:** Cook fish fillets on an oiled grate, flipping for even cooking.

ONE-POT MEALS

- **Stews or Soups:** Combine ingredients in a pot, simmering over the fire.

- **Dutch Oven Cooking:** Use a Dutch oven for casseroles, bread, or roasts over the fire.

FIRE MANAGEMENT FOR COOKING

ADJUSTING HEAT

- **Controlling Flames:** Shift vessels closer or further from flames for heat regulation.

- **Gradual Fuel Addition:** Add small fuel pieces as needed for consistent heat.

COAL COOKING

- **Using Hot Coals:** Place a grate/pan on hot coals for even heat distribution and longer cooking.

- **Covering with Ash:** Using hot ash over pots/pans creates an oven-like effect, ideal for baking.

SAFETY MEASURES

FIRE SAFETY

- **Controlled Flames:** Keep fire manageable to prevent accidents or flare-ups.

- **Extinguishing Fire:** Completely douse fire with water and stir ashes for safety.

FOOD SAFETY

- **Thorough Cooking**: Ensure food is cooked thoroughly to prevent foodborne illnesses.

- **Proper Storage**: Store cooked and uncooked food separately to prevent contamination.

Conclusion

Cooking over an open fire in the wilderness presents an enriching culinary experience. Mastery of diverse cooking methods, proper fire management, and adherence to safety measures are essential for relishing delicious meals while embracing nature's serenity.

Signaling for Help in Wilderness Emergencies

Signaling for rescue in a wilderness emergency is crucial for attracting attention and seeking help. Here's a comprehensive guide covering various effective methods to signal for rescue:

VISUAL SIGNALS

Smoke Signals:

- **Preparing a Signal Fire**: Use green vegetation or damp materials to produce thick, white smoke.

- **Signal Patterns**: Create distinctive patterns like short bursts or irregular clouds to attract attention.

Reflective Materials:

- **Signal Mirror**: Use a mirror or reflective material to reflect sunlight towards potential rescuers.

- **Flashlights/Headlamps:** Flash lights repetitively at night towards potential rescuers.

Ground Markers:

- **Rock Arrows:** Arrange rocks in arrow shapes pointing to your location.

- **Symbol Carvings:** Carve symbols or messages into the ground for visibility from the air.

AUDIBLE SIGNALS

Whistles or Horns:

- **International Distress Signal:** Blow three short blasts in succession (SOS) using a whistle or horn.

- **Consistent Signaling:** Repeat signals regularly to increase chances of being heard.

Shouting and Yelling:

- **Distinct Calls:** Shout "help" or use specific distress calls periodically.

- **Universal Signals**: Yell "Mayday" or "SOS" to convey distress effectively.

Noise-Making Devices:

- **Creating Loud Sounds**: Bang on metal objects or use whistles to create repetitive loud noises.

GROUND-TO-AIR SIGNALS

EMERGENCY SYMBOLS:

- **Ground Markings**: Create large symbols/messages using natural materials visible from the air.

- **Bright Fabric/Objects**: Lay out brightly colored clothing or items in open areas.

PRE-MADE SIGNAL PANELS OR FLAGS:

- **Prepared Materials**: Use pre-made signal panels or flags with contrasting colors to spell out distress messages or create attention-grabbing signals.

CONSIDERATIONS FOR EFFECTIVE SIGNALING

Contrasting Colors:

- **Visibility**: Use contrasting colors that stand out against the environment.

- **Visibility Angle**: Ensure signals are visible from various angles and distances.

Consistency and Repetition:

- **Regular Signaling**: Repeat signals consistently to increase noticeability.

Location Selection:

- **Visibility and Accessibility**: Choose open areas with high visibility and accessibility to rescuers.

Conclusion

Creating effective signals for rescue demands creativity, visibility, and consistency. Utilize visual, audible, and ground-to-air signaling methods to increase the chances of attracting attention and being rescued. Continuously signal for help while being prepared for potential rescue.

ATTRACTING ATTENTION IN A WILDERNESS EMERGENCY

Effectively attracting attention in a wilderness emergency demands resourcefulness and strategic implementation. Here's an extensive guide covering various techniques:

1. MIRROR SIGNALS

Using a Signal Mirror:

- **Positioning**: Hold the mirror at eye level and reflect sunlight towards potential rescuers or passing aircraft.

- **Flashing Signals**: Aim flashes towards the target in a repetitive pattern to attract attention.

2. AUDIBLE SIGNALS

Whistles, Horns, or Noise Makers:

- **Distinct Sounds**: Blow whistles or horns in sequences of three (SOS) or in a repetitive pattern.

- **Percussion Instruments**: Create loud, repetitive noises using metal objects, rocks, or logs.

Shouting and Yelling:

- **Distinct Calls**: Shout "help" or use distress calls periodically to attract attention.

- **Universal Signals**: Yell "Mayday" or "SOS" effectively conveys distress.

---

3. FIRE-BASED SIGNALS

Creating Smoke:

- **Signal Fires**: Build a smoky fire using damp materials or green vegetation during the day.

- **Smoke Patterns**: Use specific smoke patterns to signal distress.

Night Fires:

- **Bright and Continuous**: Keep the fire burning bright through the night for visual signaling.

- **Adding Fuel Gradually**: Maintain fire visibility by periodically adding fuel.

4. OTHER METHODS

Use of Bright Colors:

- **Clothing or Objects**: Display brightly colored items in open areas to stand out.

- **Bright Flags or Panels**: Use contrasting colors to create attention-grabbing signals.

Ground-Based Symbols:

- **Symbols or Markings**: Create visible symbols or messages using natural materials.

Use of Flares or Signal Rockets:

- **Visual Distress Signals**: Use handheld flares or signal rockets both day and night.

CONSIDERATIONS FOR EFFECTIVENESS

Location and Visibility:

- **High Visibility Locations**: Choose open, accessible areas for signaling.

- **Accessibility**: Signal in locations accessible to rescuers.

Consistency and Repetition:

- **Regular Signaling**: Repeat signals consistently for increased noticeability.

Timing and Persistence:

- **Continuous Signaling**: Maintain signals persistently, day and night.

Conclusion

Effectively attracting attention in a wilderness emergency involves creativity, visibility, and persistence. Utilize mirrors, audible signals, fire-based methods, bright colors, and ground-based symbols to maximize the chances of being noticed by potential rescuers. Remain vigilant, stay hopeful, and continuously signal for help while being prepared for potential rescue.

MAKING A DISTRESS CALL WITH A RADIO OR PHONE IN A WILDERNESS EMERGENCY

When facing a wilderness emergency, using a radio or phone to make a distress call can significantly aid in seeking help. Here's a comprehensive guide on how to effectively use these devices:

USING A RADIO

Emergency Channel Selection:

- **VHF Radios:** Switch to Channel 16, the international maritime distress frequency, or Channel 9 for CB radios, designated as the emergency channel.

Clear Communication:

- **Be Concise**: Use clear language and follow distress protocols like "Mayday" or "Pan-Pan" for urgency.

Information to Include:

- **Nature of Emergency**: Briefly describe the situation and the number of individuals involved.

- **Location Details**: Provide landmarks or coordinates to pinpoint your location.

USING A CELL PHONE

Call Emergency Services:

- **Dial Emergency Number**: Call 911 (or the local emergency number) and remain on the line if possible.

Provide Essential Information:

- **Location Details**: Clearly describe your location using landmarks or GPS coordinates.

- **Nature of Emergency**: Explain the situation—medical issue, being lost, or any other pertinent details.

TIPS FOR EFFECTIVE DISTRESS CALLS

Maintain Calmness:

- **Stay Composed**: Speak clearly and calmly to convey accurate information.

Repeat Information:

- **Reinforce Details**: Repeat essential information if necessary for clarity.

Signal Strength and Reception:

- **Maximize Signal**: Move to open spaces or higher ground to improve reception for radios or phones.

CONSIDERATIONS FOR WILDERNESS DISTRESS CALLS

Battery Conservation:

- **Preserve Battery Life**: Minimize unnecessary usage to conserve battery power.

Continuous Attempts:

- **Repeat Calls:** If the call doesn't connect, persistently attempt contact periodically.

Simultaneous Signaling:

- **Visual or Audible Signals:** Alongside radio or phone calls, create visual or audible signals for added visibility.

Conclusion

Making a distress call with a radio or cell phone is crucial during a wilderness emergency. Communicating essential details clearly, providing accurate location information, and following distress protocols significantly enhance the chances of receiving timely help.

Group Dynamics and Decision-Making for Kids in Outdoor Settings

GROUP DYNAMICS

Creating a Shared Purpose and Values:

- **Clear Objectives:** Define expedition goals emphasizing teamwork and collective success.

- **Embracing Values:** Encourage respect for nature, supporting peers, and taking group responsibility.

- **Inclusivity:** Foster an inclusive space, celebrating diversity and learning from varied perspectives.

Effective Communication and Conflict Resolution:

- **Active Listening:** Teach attentive listening and empathy towards diverse viewpoints.

- **Respectful Expression**: Encourage expressing thoughts respectfully even in disagreements.

- **Conflict Resolution**: Equip kids with negotiation and mediation skills for constructive conflict resolution.

Cooperation and Teamwork:

- **Task Distribution**: Equitably assign responsibilities among members for overall success.

- **Mutual Support**: Foster a positive environment with mutual encouragement and celebration of achievements.

- **Acknowledging Strengths**: Recognize individual strengths, nurturing mutual respect within the group.

Leadership and Personal Growth:

- **Encouraging Leadership**: Provide opportunities for leadership roles within the group.

- **Personal Growth**: Encourage stepping out of comfort zones and learning from outdoor experiences.

- **Reflection and Goal Setting**: Encourage self-reflection and goal setting for future leadership roles.

DECISION-MAKING

Involving Kids in Planning:

- **Seeking Input**: Actively gather ideas and suggestions from children, valuing their perspectives.

- **Decision-Making Approaches**: Teach various approaches like consensus building or majority voting.

- **Informed Decisions**: Provide relevant information for well-informed decisions about activities and challenges.

Promoting Responsible Decision-Making:

- **Considering Safety**: Emphasize safety assessment and risk evaluation in outdoor decisions.

- **Weighing Options**: Encourage understanding consequences for the group and environment.

- **Adaptability**: Teach flexibility in decision-making based on changing conditions.

Feedback and Support:

- **Constructive Feedback**: Offer constructive criticism to enhance decision-making skills.

- **Guidance**: Provide assistance when challenges arise during the outdoor experience.

- **Celebrating Success**: Acknowledge positive decision-making contributing to the adventure.

TEACHING WILDERNESS ETHICS AND LEAVE NO TRACE PRINCIPLES TO KIDS

SIGNIFICANCE OF WILDERNESS ETHICS:

1. **Responsible Enjoyment**: Ensuring wilderness enjoyment without harming its integrity.

2. **Preservation for Generations**: Safeguarding the wilderness for future appreciation.

3. **Protection of Wildlife**: Preserving wildlife and their habitats from human interference.

LEAVE NO TRACE PRINCIPLES:

- **Plan Ahead and Prepare**

- **Travel and Camp on Durable Surfaces**

- **Dispose of Waste Properly**

- **Leave What You Find**

- **Minimize Campfire Impacts**

- **Respect Wildlife**

- **Be Considerate of Others**

Tips for Instilling Wilderness Ethics in Kids:

1. **Early Introduction**: Start teaching ethics early for better understanding.

2. **Interactive Learning**: Use games, activities, and stories to engage kids.

3. **Lead by Example**: Set a good example with your own adherence to principles.

4. **Encourage Participation**: Involve kids in planning and practicing Leave No Trace principles.

Activities for Teaching Wilderness Ethics:

1. **Nature Walks**: Respect for plants and animals encountered.

2. **Campfire Building**: Safety practices and proper waste disposal.

3. **Campsite Setup**: Choosing durable sites and cleaning up trash.

4. **Litter Cleanup**: Emphasize the importance of maintaining cleanliness.

5. **Resource Utilization**: Books and videos for additional learning materials.

Exploring Different Ecosystems and Habitats

Understanding Ecosystems and Habitats:

- **Ecosystems**: Interconnected communities of living organisms and their physical surroundings.

- **Habitats**: Environments where specific organisms thrive.

Importance of Exploring Ecosystems:

1. **Understanding Diversity**: Learning inter-species interactions and environmental dynamics.

2. **Appreciating Biodiversity**: Recognizing the richness of life and its importance for global well-being.

3. **Fun and Connection**: Developing a deeper connection with nature's beauty.

Ways to Explore Ecosystems:

- **Visit Local Parks**: Interpretive centers and knowledgeable staff offer insights.

- **Outdoor Activities**: Hiking, camping, and backpacking immerse in diverse ecosystems.

- **Field Trips:** Educational trips arranged by organizations provide insights.

- **Educational Resources:** Books, documentaries, and online resources offer learning opportunities.

- **Engage with Conservationists:** Conversations with professionals provide insights into ecosystem protection.

Examples of Ecosystems and Habitats:

- **Forests:** Diverse flora and fauna coexist among trees and shrubs.

- **Grasslands:** Open landscapes with grasses and wildlife like bison.

- **Deserts:** Harsh habitats supporting specially adapted flora and fauna.

- **Wetlands:** Water-covered areas hosting diverse aquatic life.

- **Marine Ecosystems:** Oceans, reefs, and estuaries teeming with marine life.

Exploring diverse ecosystems and habitats enlightens about Earth's biodiversity, fostering appreciation while offering enjoyable experiences.

Congratulations, Young Adventurers!

As you come to the end of this handbook, you've journeyed through essential knowledge, equipping yourselves to become true wilderness experts! From crafting shelters to identifying safe food, mastering navigation to fostering teamwork, you've acquired indispensable skills for your adventures.

The wilderness awaits as a captivating playground for your exploration. With the wisdom and abilities you've gained, you're prepared to tackle any challenge that nature presents! Remember, the most potent survival tools are your creativity, bravery, and reverence for the outdoors.

Every adventure you embark upon will unveil new experiences, tales, and revelations. Pack your curiosity, keep your senses keen, and confidently embrace the wonders of the wild!

As you venture forth, share your knowledge and skills with friends and family. Together, let's cultivate a world where adventure and nature harmonize and thrive hand in hand.

Your expedition has just begun. Stay courageous, stay inquisitive, and allow the wilderness to be your greatest mentor!

Happy Exploring, Young Survivors!

Made in the USA
Monee, IL
23 February 2024

a610d15a-440e-4094-8853-12e5bc650967R01